# Sweet Blisters

*poems by*

# Phyllis St George

*Finishing Line Press*
Georgetown, Kentucky

# Sweet Blisters

## ACKNOWLEDGMENTS

I gratefully acknowledge the editors of the following journals where versions
of these poems previously appeared:

"I Went Looking for A Poem" is forthcoming in *Sinister Wisdom*, Summer
2026
"Your Hands" and "Aging Female Poet Attends Writing Retreat," *Sinister
Wisdom 117*, Summer 2020
"Half A Century" and "Hide-and-Seek 1969," *30 Poems in November! An
anthology of poems to benefit Center for New Americans*, 2013 and 2017,
respectively

Publisher: Leah Huete de Maines
Editor: Christen Kincaid
Cover Art: May Dawney
Author Photo: Terry Decker
Cover Design: Elizabeth Maines McCleavy

Order online: www.finishinglinepress.com
also available on amazon.com

Author inquiries and mail orders:
Finishing Line Press
PO Box 1626
Georgetown, Kentucky 40324
USA

# Contents

Hide-and-Seek 1969 .......................................................................... 1

Behind the Family Portrait .............................................................. 2

Catching Grasshoppers ..................................................................... 5

My Mom's Fast Hands ...................................................................... 6

My Father's Dance ............................................................................ 7

The Origin of War ........................................................................... 8

Gifts from My Mom ......................................................................... 9

In the Beginning ............................................................................ 10

Sonnet for Summer '64 .................................................................. 11

Remembering Adolescence ............................................................. 12

Square Dancing at Powder Hollow ................................................ 13

Not Leafless ................................................................................... 14

Bird Watching ............................................................................... 15

Hold Fast to Dreams ..................................................................... 16

Poem For My Grandparents ........................................................... 17

Browsing My Copy of The Norton Introduction to Literature
    from 1975 ................................................................................ 19

he .................................................................................................. 20

Volunteering at the Nursing Home ............................................... 21

Your Hands .................................................................................... 22

Working in the Connecticut Tobacco Fields ................................. 23

In Praise of My Sister .................................................................... 24

I Went Looking for a Poem ............................................................ 25

Half A Century .............................................................................. 27

Dear Niece ..................................................................................... 28

How It Is ....................................................................................... 29

Things That Raise My Blood Pressure ........................................... 30

Journey .......................................................................................... 31

March Sunrise at Patchwork Farm Retreat 2018 .......................... 32

Aging Female Poet Attends Writing Retreat .................................. 33

## Hide-and-Seek 1969
*For Galway Kinnel's Hide-and-Seek 1933*

The yard around the house
both sides of the viburnum bushes
with the front steps as home.

After the cookout and cleanup
and the watermelon seed spitting contest
as soon as it got dark.

When the person who was "it"
found one of us, there was a race
to home to beat the "it" person.

Winning was everything to my
four cousins, brother, sister, and me.
No one wanted to be last.

The older boys played rough
pushed me aside to tag home first.
I made peace with losing.

The attention of being looked for
made getting knocked down worth it.
I gave back what I could.

The adults were busy drinking beer
when my cousin Jon
cracked his chin open on the concrete steps.

My parents insisted we change home base
to the maple tree in the front yard
away from the steps.

I said the cement wasn't the problem.
I wanted to say more, much more, but Jon
was being put in the car to go to the hospital.

If I close my eyes I still see
the white of his jawbone
and all the blood.

## Behind the Family Portrait

A hot and muggy August day is ending, and I sit on the warmed
ledge of the street drain. I drop stones through the steel grates
of the gutter and listen for the *plop*
while waiting for my father to come home in the car with strange
men.

Cars rush by on the busier main street. I peer between my bony
knees to watch as each stone breaks the dark surface of the
water with a *plunk*. A car pulls off the main road
crunching the gravel at the top of my street, startling me.

My father steps out and says "Hi." The men are laughing but
go quiet when they see me. The car door shuts with a thud. My
father carries his jacket and tie, shirt open. I watch the car amble
back onto the main road as my father starts out towards our
house. His hard heels crunch the sandy dirt, and I half-hop, half-
run in my bare feet on the hot asphalt to keep up.

At our driveway, my father remarks "The grass needs cutting,
and the weeds need picking," and sighs. I regard the puffy white
balls of dandelion seeds with delight but am forbidden to pick
them and blow them into the air. My father says this makes more
weeds.

Up the driveway and into the back door and my mother calls my
brother and sister from the T.V. and we eat. Macaroni salad, hot
dogs, and corn-on-the-cob. It is too hot to eat much. I am eager
to go play. I rush outside. My mother and father clear the table,
do the dishes. The late-day-sun is still toasty on my head. I sit
where our lawn meets the street—no curb—and I draw in the
dirt with a cigarette butt and erase with my feet—bottoms black
as licorice. The screen door rattles open and slams. My parents
come outside. My mother sits on the steps, smoking. My father
is down on one knee like a statue or a football player resting one
arm on a bent leg with that hand holding a fistful of weeds and
the other hand pulling at the lawn. He works methodically, and I
come to help him, but my hands are not strong enough. The

weed snaps at the base leaving the root to grow and haunt my
father again.

He tells me I cannot help because I do not do it right. The
neighborhood kids appear, and I go get my kickball from my
cluttered bedroom closet. We play in the idle street, marking off
bases with rocks that write on asphalt. The bigger kids come from
the other end of the street and tell us what to do. My father stops
mowing on and off to cheer us on, and I wonder if he would
rather play with us than mow.

The whine of his mower and the screams of the kids intermingle.
The sun falls into the woods beyond our house. The branches
of the trees pull it down and the road under my feet cools
to pleasantly warm. The streetlights turn on like dots of
light marching forward to absorb the darkness. All over the
neighborhood, bells ring, names are called. It is time to go in.

The bathwater is ready for my sister and me. Stripping down, we
throw our clothes at each other. My undershirt lands in the water.
We are giggling and my mother yells—in the tub quick—me in
the back, my sister at the front near the faucets. We splash and
make more bubbles stealing them from each other in handfuls.
My father joins us to wash our backs. The water turns brown. We
get out clean.

It is my brother's turn with fresh water. Afterwards my brother,
sister, and I fight for a place on the couch to watch *Get Smart* and
*I Dream of Jeanie*. Then bedtime, groans, and a march to the
bathroom sink to brush our teeth. My brother and I spit in the
sink aiming at each other's hands and toothbrushes until my
mother says "Enough."

My father gathers us to continue the journey down the hall. My
brother breaks off to his room, my sister and I to ours. We say
our prayers—"Now I lay me down to sleep"—and kiss
goodnight.

We laugh and giggle long after my parents are settled in the living room, and they must yell to us: "Go to sleep."

Later that night, my father paces the house. I am afraid.

In the morning, I practice forgetting.

## Catching Grasshoppers

My technique was to follow one
as it jumped and grab it mid-air
then hold it for a second,
open my hands and throw it at the sky.

They pee on your hands when you catch them.
Reddish yellow streaks across your palms.
We always released them.
The thrill was being quick enough.

We went to the field behind our houses.
The sun, the pre-summer breeze, the smell
of dirt and a mess of grasshoppers.
The whole afternoon beckoned.

My mother saw us leaving the meadow, and called
*You're going to be late.* She got the car
and drove me to school. I made it to my classroom
one second before the bell.

My soul flourished in the fresh air
while my heart loved school's attention
and approval. Why couldn't we go
to school on rainy days only?

I sit in my sun-filled living room
capturing poems and releasing
them. With the windows open
it is almost like being outside.

## My Mom's Fast Hands

Thwick thwick thwick so quick
as she clipped the clothespins on the folded edges
of sheets, towels, shirts, skirts,
blouses, trousers, and undershirts.
In no time she emptied
the white, wicker basket.
Wash after wash, thwick thwick thwick.

Wish wish wish I wanted
to stay young and foolish.
Be a rock star, an actor, a writer.
No husband, no children
an auntie to my sister's kids.
My mother saw me as a quandary.
I craved her approval wish wish wish.

To this day I don't know whether
she loved me. I only know she tried tried tried

## My Father's Dance

my father's dance was an accident
while putting his daughters to bed
he twirled around without incident
until he stumbled and hit his head

on the door and we wanted more
every night we anticipated his silliness
until for him it became a bore
we didn't know it was from tipsiness

I weep now when I think
of all we didn't know
our flesh so young and pink
as he would come and go

how can I lose this curse
and live a joyous life
free my mind in rhymed verse?
choosing happy the best advice

when he came late at night
it was me he preferred
I knew this dance wasn't right
do I dare write an afterword?

## The Origin of War

Said the cat,

"You itch me
with your bites
in my flesh.
Yours is a system
of jump and crawl.
There is you
the catapult
and there is you
the stone.
You love nestling in my fur.
Your deep longing
like the calling
of that first scent,
bee to flower."

Said the flea,

"I have seen you
furry snob
in that business
in your litter box.
It's known,
little know-it-all, you
run the house
from the couch.
You could be a princess.
You scratch at me,
like a desperado or an addict.
You are no flower and
I am no bee."

**Gifts from My Mom**

Cinnamon sprinkled on leftover pie crust for her children on a late afternoon. Books read on the couch right after bathtime. Clean sheets warm from the iron every week but more if they were sick. Thanksgiving meals cooked all morning. Christmas presents wrapped and waiting. Slices of cheese in the car on a long ride. Hand-sewn Easter outfits. Mercurochrome applied gently to scraped knees. Hot baths drawn before bedtime. Braided and curled hair for school days. Chaperone for the Girl Scout trip to New York City. Help with art projects and tough homework. Lessons about not littering and being polite.

waves pound and bash
erosion of the spirit
stars flicker out

## In the Beginning

3 o'clock in the morning
your father staring down at you
a girl just starting puberty

Atoms clash against atoms

Now you are separate, damaged,
not like the other girls, an oddity
Your brother and his friends
are stronger, meaner

You can't fight them off

when you've been slipped Valium
from one of the boy's mother's scripts

when you weigh less
than one hundred pounds

And now you're unhappy as a red rash
angry as a batted-at hornet
full of razors and daggers

Give them hell

## Sonnet for Summer '64

fireflies take over the field at night
tame the darkness with their blinking
the air shudders with flickering light
and I hold my breath without thinking

God designed a miraculous creature
tiny electric lights mating in my sight
teach me about God better than any preacher
brighten the scary woods at night

I drop self-pity and misery
in awe of God's ornaments
how long have they been at this trickery
as God's humble instruments

Light pollution is killing these insects
I don't know how to pay my last respects

## Remembering Adolescence

I drop my rear
on my unmade bed
clenching my fists hard,
leaving four moon-shaped
dents in my palm.

Hot tears roll down
my flushed face.
One tear hesitates
on the edge of my lips.
I lick it and taste salt.

My glasses are wet
and my view is blurred
like a car windshield
in a downpour.
I slip them off my face.

I feel each tear
trace a path across my face
so lightly it tickles,
and the pleasure of my own
sorrow comforts me.

**Square Dancing at Powder Hollow**

I had breasts but I wasn't a woman yet. My parents dropped me off at Powder Hollow barn to learn how to square dance. I was a shy animal tending to avoid humans and predators. The dancers mistook my shyness for snobbery, and nobody talked to me. The first time I danced for a whole call my heart pounded, and I tingled all over. I was with adults, and the man who became my partner wasn't a boy at all. He liked me and at the end of the summer said he'd come to see me when I was eighteen. He was in his twenties, a little effeminate, and he lived with his mother. He did come, and I felt and looked like a woman, but I wouldn't come out of my room, and he left, never to return. In the time between square dancing and his visit I renounced the idea of marriage to my grandmother. I felt triumphant claiming my freedom from men, society, and marriage. "Oh my God," she kept repeating. I'd had enough dancing with my father for a lifetime.

## Not Leafless

What is the requisite for a mother's love?
Will a child grow golden without her love?

Life's sap is nipped and stems itself when
a robin from the blue egg withholds love.

We heard library books read at bedtime.
Pressed snug to your side we beheld your love.

Orange red yellow leaves fall. Nothing can
keep leaf to branch, not even autumn love.

From leftover pie dough and cinnamon
you created a treat. Behold your love!

Haustorium root sucks nutrients to
the parasite mistletoe. Toxic love!

Your silent treatment like a cord choked me.
A strong-willed child survives. We forgot love.

Ragweed and crabgrass are weeded out
They fail without a gardener's love.

So tender to my sister and brother.
For the gay child conditional love.

Zero conditional Laws of Nature:
When plants aren't watered, they die despite love.

Some days I want to cut myself or die.
Who could transform her life raised on such love?

My name Phyllis means leafy foliage and green bough.
I sprouted leaves even lacking your love.

## Bird Watching

his bright blue and white visage stark
against the green foliage
with that punk blue hair style
a big white belly, black streaks on his face
geometric markings on his wings and tail
he is conceited and proud
the birdfeeder is meant only
for him and he cocks his head
jauntily to one side as he dominates
the birdbath he is one of the few birds
I can identify and I love his joie de vivre

## Hold Fast to Dreams

You wanted to be a spy, you madcap schemer.
Not marriage, not children, but travel.
You think you're too old, too sick
to still dream?

Dreams become screams if stifled
Write a spy novel and live your fantasy
Fix all the world's problems in a book

## Poem For My Grandparents

grandmothers are the tenderest
        grandfathers are rugged burlap bags
flowers in the garden, but they
        and teachers of skullduggery
lose their petals fast,
        they fall asleep in stuffed chairs
and they are gone with the
        watch sports and ignore everyone
spring breezes too late to
        pass on their sins to the fifth generation
realize how much their love lifts
        yet grandmothers outlive them

my maternal grandmother was hardy
        my maternal grandfather died at 32
lavender, fragrant and perky
        after fathering seven children
she lived faraway in California
        my aunts and uncles and mother
her visits were oases in a long drought
        he was a jaunty stockbroker dressed
of neglect and inattention
        in suits in all the photos of him
I wanted to live with her
        I wish I had met him

my paternal grandmother was thistle
        my paternal grandfather smoked and gambled
prickly, beautiful, and strong
        liked to sit outside in his undershirt
she cooked delicious Saturday dinners
        taught us to play cards and laugh at troubles
and believed putting diapers on infants
        couldn't tell my sister from me

caused them to poop in their pants
                 ate the turkey drumstick on Thanksgiving
she was born in Canada
                 and died in his seventies from diabetes

both grandmothers wanted me
                 I became a drunk like one grandfather
to get married and settle down
                 and a diabetic like the other
my soul was too wild for that life
                 I have their natures for trouble and
and I knew I would mimic
                 may live longer than both
my parent's marriage
                 they died too young
and live unhappily
                 I wish I could go back

**Browsing My Copy of The Norton Introduction to Literature from 1975**

Emily was patient; she spent all day watching spiders and snakes and worms and birds. Frost closely observed nature and spied God's design. Whitman compared his errant soul to the methodical spider. Even Lowell saw God's work in the spider's efforts. Not so many spider poems now. Maybe there are fewer spiders. Are we better at dusting and cleaning our homes or do we use too many pesticides? Could we still come upon a giant white spider web in a corner of a barn?


Poets, read the masters
invigorate with solitude
seek spiders and webs

**he**

his penis has one long hair
extending from it
he is very hairy
everywhere like a bear and
he sheds on my bed
he is more
experienced than me
and is gentle
he says "I don't mind
that you are with women too."
he wants to marry and have
no children
he is passive-aggressive and has
mommy issues
we never make it
past the first year

## Volunteering at the Nursing Home

I hold your hand
as you lie in this hospital bed.
You think I am your daughter.
You tell me you are sorry.
I squeeze your hand.
You say now
that I am twenty and grown up,
you hope things are going well for me—

your daughter should be here
to hear your confession of guilt,
to clear your conscience.
I tell you I am not your daughter.
"Do you want me to call your daughter?"
I ask and hold my breath.

You falter, confused,
and when I say nothing,
you continue about
how much you love me, what
a beautiful girl I was, how you
didn't mean to ever hurt me.

You could be my father.
If I called your daughter
would she laugh a bitter laugh
and say, "So what!"
If I asked to trade fathers
would she say
"He's not my father anymore.
I left him long ago."

I wonder what kind of monster you were,
and why now, too late,
you choose to ask forgiveness

## Your Hands

Your hands I remember,
though they never touched me.
The tanned skin,
the gleaming pink nails
with white half-moons,
the delicate muscles and
strong knuckles
gestured
as I listened to you tell us
what you did for a living.

No one else spoke until you finished,
and then everyone mentioned the heat
and humidity and *why don't we all*
*go skinny dipping in the lake?*

The cold water refreshed us
and I watched you leave
with a pretty girl
who told me
she was in real estate.

## Working in the Connecticut Tobacco Fields

Early morning
the clay soil is damp
from the morning dew.

The wide tobacco leaves flap
against my legs
as I walk down the row
carrying my string
tying the plants
to the wire above them.

My fingers are stiff,
fumbling with loose string
moving of its own accord.

The nicotine on the sticky leaves
pulls the hairs on my hand
turning them black.

Bent bodies across the field
work with flowing motion, up and down.

Overhead, netting undulates
in the morning breeze.

The string is wet,
slices my hand, opening cuts
that have scabbed and bled over and over.

Tobacco is my summer job and I dream
all day of playing tennis at Wimbledon.

### In Praise of My Sister

*after Wistawa Szymborska's In Praise of My Sister*

My sister doesn't write poems,
but I think she could write a memoir.
She likes me to read my poems to her.
Our father didn't write poems,
but he liked mine
at least the ones I showed him.
Our mother didn't write poems.
Our cousin may have written one or two,
but it was just to show me up.

My sister doesn't have dusty boxes
from high school and college
with old writing in them.
She isn't revising poems
from thirty years ago.
She raised a family and runs a household.
She's a nurse and works long hours.
She makes a delicious pot roast.

There are many nurses in our
extended family but no
other poets. There won't be
another poet for a long time.

My sister writes me postcards
when on vacation telling
what she's doing and see you soon.

I write postcards back
little prose poems
asking for forgiveness
for not marrying
for not having children
I get them back return to sender

## I Went Looking for a Poem

I went looking for a poem in the darkness of my childhood
bedroom
>I looked under the bed and saw myself at three huddled
>in fear among the dust bunnies
>I looked in the closet and saw myself at seven on my
>knees praying for someone to help

I went looking for a poem in the darkness of my childhood, and
I left it there

I went looking for a poem at twenty on the dirty streets of a
college town
>I looked in the bars and saw myself falling off a stool,
>puking in the bathroom, and going home with people I
>didn't know
>I looked in the classroom and saw a sad loner wasting
>talent and brains on fear and worry
>I looked across the quadrangle into the night and saw
>the gothic chapel looming over my head as I walked
>alone

I went looking for a poem in the darkness of a city campus, and I
started to write poetry

I went looking for a poem at thirty in the hallways of a Fortune
500 company
>I looked at the cubicles and saw myself hunched over my
>desk with fear and trembling
>I looked in the cafeteria and saw myself eating and
>gaining weight
>I looked at my coworkers sitting nearby and saw cruelty

I went looking for a poem in the bottom of a beer, and I stopped
writing

I went looking for a poem at forty in my newfound sobriety
>I looked at the lesbians in Northampton and saw myself
>at last
>I looked at my coworkers still making fun of me and saw
>myself feel pity for them

> I looked at my fellow writers in my writing group and
> saw talent and fulfillment

I went looking for a poem in the middle of my life, and I began writing again

I went looking for a poem at fifty in the yellow flowers of my garden and found blue bachelor buttons

> I looked at the walls of my home and saw myself
> disabled from work before fifty
> I looked at friends still drinking and saw myself grateful
> to be sober and alive
> I looked at my eating and saw myself substituting food
> for booze

I went looking for a poem as a sober person and heard my voice getting stronger

I went looking for a poem at sixty in writing workshops and residencies

> I looked at my future and saw writing as my salvation
> I looked at my poetry and saw myself grateful to be
> published
> I looked at my family and saw my parents pass on

I went looking for a poem among other writers and found my family replaced

## Half a Century

Shouldn't wisdom come in half a century?
Shouldn't understanding and faith be rewards
of a tough, long trudge?
After the bitter apple seeds are spit out—

After the same argument spoken repeatedly
  in hundreds of versions
  no longer makes sense—

After each tiny hurt and disappointment held onto
  like a lifejacket
  finally deflate—

After the long-term companions of anger, rage, and
frustration
  invite their friends
  migraine headaches, panic attacks, and depression—

After the object of rage and perpetrator of sadistic violence
  becomes disabled
  and wheelchair-bound—

Even after the nails are driven
  into the wood
  and the whole business is finished—

Shouldn't you know it's time?
Time to leap and freefall,
letting life take you where it will,
choosing happiness at last?

**Dear Niece**

Thank you
for bringing me
two pumice stones
from Bermuda
I did not want
to burden you
with shopping for trinkets.

Walking the beach you chose one stone
a small, shapely, white mass
smooth, with protruding lumps and a pinched underbelly
left at your feet, like a discarded potter's scrap.

The other
just the stone I would picture if someone said "pumice stone"
airy and delicately light
with a pocked surface and sandy coloring,
and when I rub my thumb over this stone,
flakes and specks of it fall on my clothes.

Over years of aunt and niece
talks and calls
defining
bare white legs now covered with dark hair
the first red menstrual blood staining the back of your pants
lined notebooks covered with boys' names
eyes wide from learning
life's events both abrasive and smooth
molded, shaped, and weathered

**How It Is**
    *after Arthur Sze*

How good breakfast tastes when you wake up famished
How the blood rushes through your veins after a 45-minute bike
ride

How you want to melt into the floor when you make a social
blunder
How satisfying it feels to hug a large friend

How scared you are when walking in the dark in a strange city
How much you miss your dead mother

How easy it is to ignore a homeless panhandler
How guilty you feel when cancelling plans with a friend

How much your obesity bothers you
How you chew the same piece of gum for hours

How wonderful chocolate feels in your mouth
How much you come alive in the sunshine

How adult you felt after making your first pot of tea
How welcoming lotion feels on your dry feet

How invincible you are after drinking whiskey
How invisible you come to be as you age

How much fun it is to play with a four-year-old
How the bartender ignores you after you've drank too much

Isn't it great to be alive?

## Things That Raise My Blood Pressure

Salty food. Pedestrians who spit on my sidewalk. Birds who poop on my car. The snowplow that adds hard-packed snow to the end of my driveway after I've shoveled it clear. Neighbors who toss cigarette butts on my lawn. Dust that collects on my floor. Unexplained diarrhea. People who talk during a presentation. People who don't wipe down the machine after exercising. Smokers in my airspace. Pens that don't write. My car when it doesn't start. Unsigned notes. Medicine that makes my mouth dry. Unexplained rashes. Dirty fingernails on acquaintances. Hairdressers who clip my ear with their scissors. Toenail fungus. People who lose their glasses and other possessions constantly. People who lie. Arguments over nothing. People with very thin arms. Loud, blasting music on a beautiful spring day. People who don't flush after using a public toilet. Shopping carts left next to my car. Relatives who never forget something regrettable I did. Polka dot pants. Bright orange lipstick.

**Journey**

I'm prepared to start out go round the corner half a block to the store. Instead, photos and postcards on my lap, I step into my former travels—Ayer's Rock now Uluru. I followed painted white *footprints* climbing from the bottom to the top. Uluru is holy land to the local Aboriginal tribe. *Now you can't climb Uluru. I didn't know then.* Wait, there's Tivoli, bright and sparkly at night. I'm twenty again riding the roller coaster facing fear and letting my heart pound—cross the street and I'm a teenager at Lenin's Tomb in Red Square gawking up at St. Basil's Cathedral, such an architectural beauty that the architect was blinded to keep it unique. Now when I see the domes, I think of chocolate candy kisses. Lenin looked so alive in 1972 with the hairs on his hand standing up—I'd never seen anything like it. *How much money did it cost to entomb and enshrine a non-capitalist?* The wind and snow beat on my picture window. My neck aches, the forced hot air has just gone on. *What year is it? How old am I?* I'm on the couch wondering if there is anyone left to call.

winter storm outside
picture window protects me
I remember Spring

## March Sunrise at Patchwork Farm Retreat 2018

Black branches are lit in an orange-red stripe across the horizon. The dark blue clouds lift to reveal more pink and yellow in the widening ribbon. Sky lightens to a muted blue. White patches appear, openings for the sun to emerge. Orange sun breaks too strong for my eyes. The birds are calling out. The light edges into my room urging me to start a poem. "Here you are," day says. "Awake at dawn. Alive. Write your joy." Only half a poem comes as my muse settles among the black limbs and orange sky. I've made a start and close my eyes for repose.

birds sing poems from
the orange-black horizon
only I can hear

## Aging Female Poet Attends Writing Retreat

*After Margaret Atwood's Aging Female Poet Sits
on the Balcony*

The late autumn trees lose their last leaves fast
to the strong gusts of wind this first writing day.

They fly like little yellow birds from the branches
off the mountain to another land for forgotten things.

The aging female poet gazes out the window at the
landscape and writes her last poems, perhaps, as

light blue hills hold the distance down, and the sun sets.
While her blood flows quick she will sing of

trees and birds, and as she ages what will she dream of?
When her sight fades with the afternoon light

will she write from memory or fear?
Crisp apples will trigger her best poems,

and she will hear what she can
of the gales and the spirits of the night.

Her childhood haunts will flicker past, and the deep
scent of pine trees will linger.

## With Thanks

I am grateful to the following writer's organizations and communities for teaching me the craft of poetry and supporting my writing:

2023 Pioneer Valley Writers' Workshop 10-Month Manuscript Program and my co-participants, especially the Extension Group through 2024;

Straw Dog Writers Guild for granting me a retreat where many of these poems were first conceived;

Fine Arts Work Center for its summer workshops;

Juniper Summer Writing Institute at UMASS Amherst where my poems were workshopped.

I thank my writing teachers who influenced me:

Carolyn Zaikowski, my 10-Month Manuscript instructor;

Gail Thomas who reviewed the manuscript in its early form;

Blair Hurley, Carol Edelstein, Dara Wier, Doug Anderson, Ellen Bass, Finn Burnett, Joy Baglio, Julia Cameron, Melanie Brooks, Nick Flynn, Patricia Lee Lewis, Rebecca Hart Olander, Robin Barber, Sarah Jane Cody, and Yona Harvey, my workshop teachers over the years.

I am grateful to the many writers who I've been in workshops with. A big shout-out to the Orange Room group who gave feedback on my poems.

Thanks to the following people for their early encouragement:

Patricia Lee Lewis and Jacqueline Sheehan of Straw Dog Writers Guild;

Carol Edelstein of Gallery of Readers;

Cobi for inspiring me to start writing again and for reviewing the manuscript;

My high school English teacher, Mrs. Muriel H, for her belief in my writing.

Many thanks to:

My mother for reading to me every night of my childhood;

My sister for being a good friend and giving me a niece and a nephew;

My sponsor, Sue, for her continuing support and encouragement.

**Phyllis St. George** is a poet, artist, and filmmaker living in Western Massachusetts. She received a B.A. in economics from Trinity College in Hartford, Connecticut. Phyllis traveled extensively when younger and worked in Denmark, Washington, D.C., and Australia. Her work history includes Connecticut tobacco fields and an assembly line at a tool-packing factory. For many years, she solved bugs in COBOL programs at a financial services company.

Her short story, "View from the Watchtower," is featured in *Anthology 5* of Running Wild Press. Her poetry has appeared in the *Hiram Poetry Review* and *Sinister Wisdom*. Her villanelle, "Last-Minute Temptation," won 3rd Place in the 2019 Palm Beach Poetry Festival Tech Effect Poetry Contest.

She produced and directed two short films, *Plastics* and *The Therapy Killings*, accepted at the Downtown Boca Festival and the Outside the Box Bakersfield Film Festival, respectively. Her short film *Plastics* won an Award of Merit for her leading actor in the March 2011 Best Shorts Competition.

Her digital artwork "Monsters in the Deep" is found in the *Bonemilk Collective Vol II* by Gutslut Press.

She enjoys playing pickle ball and taking walks.

*Sweet Blister*s is her first poetry collection.

| | |
|---|---|
| pinterest | pstgeorge0559 |
| Facebook | Phyllis St George |
| Instagram | phyllis.j.stgeorge.1 |
| tumblir | fiercepoetfilmmaker |
| LinkedIn | phyllis-st-george-poet-and-writer |
| bluesky | @phyllisstgeorge.bsky.social |